Contents

about
m e

Hi,

My name is Jack, an odd choice for a girl, I know, but it stuck after a college night out and it's stayed with me ever since! I am now working my way through my 40s and trying hard to be a cool mum and wife and run a business all at the same time!

In 2014 I started my Prop Hire and Wedding Styling business named Pretty Quirky Hire after I was subject to getting a bad case of the wedding blues!

I very quickly missed the whole process of planning and organising my wedding day and I felt it left a hole that I needed to fill. I wanted all that excitement back of bringing something magical together.

So over a few months, I bought a few vintage crates and suitcases and kept them in my garage and when I felt I had enough I started to hire them out to other couples. Nine years later I am proud to say the business has grown into its showroom, with over £20K worth of stock available to hire.

It is always an absolute privilege to be asked to be involved in someone's wedding day and one I am very grateful for. I still get excited and I am hugely passionate about delivering the best days to all my clients, no matter how big or small a touch I bring.

You see a wedding is a momentous occasion in anyone's life. For most of us, it is a day that has been thought about since childhood. A single day that has been dreamed about and one that will be cherished for the rest of your life.

The reason I decided to write this book is to share all the knowledge I have learnt styling many different weddings throughout my time in the industry. I want to give you the wisdom to make good decisions about your wedding decoration. I want you to know how to make your venues look fabulous, but also guarantee that it will save you valuable time and most definitely your hard-earned money too.

I am thrilled that you have bought my book so we can start on your wedding decoration planning together.

Jack x

So you said "YES"

Welcome to the whole new world of weddings

They finally asked and now you can't stop looking at that ring on your finger?

I remember being in this exact position, it is such a lovely place to be, daydreaming about the upcoming wedding of your dreams and creating something fabulous for your friends and family to enjoy.

Planning your wedding day should be one of the most exciting times in your life.

Weddings are now so varied and your options are so vast. No longer are we shackled to a Cadbury's purple reception room in our local Social Club. It is your chance to go wild and at the start of your wedding journey, you should do exactly that. Take the time to look at absolutely everything there is on offer to you. Look at all the things you like, love and even things you have never even thought about. You may just surprise yourself and find something you never knew existed. It can be a real thrill of a ride and one you will remember forever, bringing you lots of joy and wonderful memories.

What to
EXPECT

Many of you may already have some knowledge about planning a wedding. You may have helped with family or friends' weddings. However, until you do it with your own emotions invested in it, I don't think we ever really know what is fully in store for us and what it entails to bring such a momentous day together.

It can be an overwhelming and daunting task, but it is like anything new, it takes a while to find your feet and feel comfortable in your new surroundings.

Very quickly you will find yourself submerged in everything there is to do with weddings. Everywhere you turn, something wedding-related will be staring back at you. Take inspiration from all areas of life, but don't let it start to consume you. Try to stay focused on the task at hand and what you are trying to achieve.

There will, of course, come a point when eventually you will want to start narrowing down your options. Make sure you do some of the window shopping first though, otherwise you may be thrown off track further down the line.

Choosing a VENUE

Choosing a venue is essential before you can start thinking about what decoration you may require. You may already have somewhere in mind, or you may need to do some groundwork to find the perfect setting for your wedding day.

Before you start looking at any venues ask yourselves a few things that will help narrow your search.

What type of ceremony do you want?
How many guests will be attending?
Where is the ideal location?
What can you realistically afford to pay?

Sit down together as a couple to take the time to answer these questions properly. Then you can move to the next exciting step of looking for your dream venue.

Choosing a VENUE

The internet will be your friend in searching for potential venues. Ask friends for recommendations, they may know of somewhere that may not even be on your radar. Social media is also a good place to source from too. There are lots of wedding forums on Facebook but my favourite place to source from is Instagram. This can be done by either typing directly into the search bar or you can search by the location tab too.

Construct a list of potential venues that fit your criteria. Then make bookings to go and see them. Then you can go and get a real feel for what they have to offer.

I strongly believe that when you visit a venue, you should be drawn to the feeling it gives you. If you are visiting a venue and it makes you feel like it could potentially be the one, then start to scratch the surface a little more. Take in the surroundings and have a nosey at all the areas you and your guests would use on the day. Also try and get a good feel for the staff working at the venue. You may well end up having a relationship with these people, working with them over the next year or so, therefore it is important that you feel comfortable talking to them and confident that they are going to give you top service throughout your wedding journey.

Durng your visit it is always a good idea to take photos or videos, this is so you can refer back to them, either to swoon over them or to compare! Take notes on the information you collect too, you are likely to be in a state of awe so you are bound to forget things once you leave.

There will be many questions you will want to ask, but for a start here are a few essential ones I would ask.

- What dates do you have available?
- Can the venue hold my ceremony and reception?
- How many guests can the venue accommodate for both the day and the evening?
- Is there any accommodation available?
- What are the catering options?
- Are there any decor restrictions?

I think this is a good start to getting to understand if the venue would work for you. Most venues will tell you everything you need to know without you having to ask, but if you do come up with other questions do not be afraid to ask them. If they are important to you they will be more than happy to answer them for you.

Quick

TIP

Before we get started, I just wanted to say -

Please do not allow yourself to feel pressured into any decision-making by anyone. Everyone is entitled to their opinion and believe me everyone will try and give you theirs, but this is going to be your day and it should be tackled and planned your way. If it does not feel right in your gut, then listen to that. You will know what you are comfortable with and what you are not.

Where to Start

We all know from the very beginning that we want a beautiful wedding day, but knowing quite how to approach it and where to start can prove difficult.

For the last nine years, I have taken all my clients through a simple, but easy-to-understand step-by-step process on how to approach their wedding decoration. This process has proven to help lots of couples throughout my years in the wedding industry. Couples will often comment on how going through my steps awakens them to what is important.

I originally devised this process to make my own life easier when discussing decoration with all of my clients. What I very quickly realised was that it also made it so much clearer for them too. It helped them to know where wedding decorations will be needed within each of their wedding venues. The great thing about this simple process is that it can be easily adapted to every type of venue. There will always be some venues that may require more attention and there will always be some that require a lot less. However, my Simple Guide should give you a very strong foundation to get you started on any venue. It has proved so helpful, to so many, that it is for this exact reason I wanted to share it with you too.

The whole guide has been created and centred around your wedding guests needs. This may not have been the approach you had thought about until now, but I strongly believe that thinking about your wedding decoration from this perspective, will mean that you make your wedding guests' comfort a priority. This is extremely important, as guests will only have a great time if they feel at ease.

Putting yourself completely in your wedding guests' shoes can help identify what decoration is required. After all, it is for their appreciation that we like to enhance our venues with decorations in the first place.

We certainly will not be compromising any of the decoration by doing it this way, we are just considering all the people that will be in the heart of it and putting them at the forefront of our minds helps to create a perfect wedding day.

Once you get started on the guide, you will see how this will simplify the whole process for you. I promise that following my simple steps will make your wedding planning far less stressful and give you back precious time and I guarantee it will save you money if you follow it properly.

Together we are going to work our way through and around your chosen venue, so we can identify where your venue needs our attention.

In my view, there are seven areas that we need to consider when planning your wedding decoration. Giving these areas the attention they require, will ensure your wedding day will run smoothly, as well as look beautiful.

These key areas are all spaces where your decoration can be added. We are going to take the time to go through each of these areas carefully. We will identify each one separately throughout the book and work out what it is you may need to get each space to look incredible.

Of course, there will always be more you can do and always more you can enhance. The trick is knowing when enough is enough. Getting the balance of decoration in your venue can be tricky, but my fail-safe plan will cover everything you should need.

Areas to CONSIDER

Area 01
LOCATION & PARKING

I know this seems an unlikely area to consider first when it comes to decorating your wedding day, but it is the very first place your guests will get an insight into what the day will bring for them.

Trying to ensure guests arrive on time for your wedding day is important. Nobody likes being late for any event, especially for someone's wedding day. You can help prevent this by giving your guests clear directions to where your wedding venue is. This should ideally be done at the time when they receive their invitations, so they have plenty of time to investigate where they need to go.

Remind yourself of your first visit to your venue,
Was the venue easy to locate?
Did you get lost?
Was it unclear on arrival where to go next?

If you are answering, "Yes" to any of these questions, then most certainly your guests will also have the same struggles. We do not want anyone to feel flustered because they cannot find where they should be. Remember that one of your aims should be to keep all your guests comfortable and relaxed, so they enjoy the day too. Ensuring they know where to go is the very start of this.

LOCATION & PARKING

Once your guests have arrived at the venue they will then need to locate the car park and familiarise themselves with their new surroundings. Ask yourself what the signage is like at your venue. Is it signposted to where your guests are expected to go next?

This may be where you first need to introduce some personal decoration. Some signs or a welcome board can make all the difference at this point. Whatever you decide is appropriate for this area you need to make sure it is visible as well as weatherproof.

When we arrive in new territory, we sometimes do not see what is right in front of us, so making your signs stand out a little is important. The use of a balloon or some ribbon tied to a neighbouring tree branch can just help to catch the attention of a lost eye and can aid so much. Try to avoid signs being at ground level, ideally they need to be in the eye line so that they are seen. Often easels are used to promote your signs, just always make sure they are sturdy enough to hold what they need to and are also the correct size. You do not want a huge easel for a small sign, or vice versa.

LOCATION & PARKING

Signs should not just stop at the car park, we want your guests to comfortably find their way to where they should be throughout the whole day. Provide as much signage as you think is required.

Giving your guests direction will give them some order, which at the beginning of the day is needed. Ask your venue if they have any easels or blackboards that could assist you with this. Larger venues are likely to already have lots of signs, but it is still nice to have personalised signage.

There are many options for how to create your signs in many different materials. It is something you could do yourself or if you are not confident in being creative you could get a professional to do them for you. Perhaps you are great at designing on a screen and then you could take your design to a printing company. The options are open but I think whatever you choose it will not only look lovely on the day but provide a practical use too.

Make Notes
LOCATION & PARKING

Area 02
ORDER OF THE DAY

An order of the day is a brief timeline which outlines the timings of events during the whole of your wedding day. I always suggest to my clients that they should have their order of the day on display because part of your guests feeling comfortable is them having a little insight into what is going on throughout their time with you on this special day. This list will enable them to know if they have time, for instance, to go and check in their bags at reception or even if they have time for another drink at the bar. Giving them that information can make them feel more content in their surroundings.

This should be displayed clearly and throughout the whole day. Remember it is only a brief outline you don't have to write down every detail. Follow my steps on the next page for how to work out your order of the day.

Order of the day
Example

A typical order of the day:

1:30 pm.	Ceremony
2:00 pm.	Drinks Reception & Photos
4:30 pm.	Wedding Breakfast
6:30 pm.	Speeches
7:00 pm.	Evening Guests Arrive
7:30 pm.	Cake Cutting/ First Dance
9:00 pm.	Evening Food
Midnight.	Home Time

How to make
your own

Working out your timings for your order of the day is fairly simple. Everyone's order of the day will start with their ceremony time.

When you book your ceremony be mindful of what the day holds. The earlier you make it, the more money you will have to potentially spend on food and entertainment to keep guests happy.

I think that a 1/2 pm wedding is best for everyone. It gives the bridal party plenty of time to get ready in the morning with hair and make-up. It is also likely that your guests will have eaten lunch before they arrive, meaning they won't be hungry too early and they will have lined their stomachs ahead of a day's drinking, which is always a good plan.

Ceremony: 1:30 pm
I would suggest a ceremony time of 1:30 pm, this would then go at the top of your timeline. A ceremony lasts on average around 30 minutes, which considering it is the most important part of your whole wedding day it doesn't last very long.

Drinks Reception: 2:00 pm

The next step of your timeline would be your drinks reception and possibly canapes, although canapes are not necessarily needed with a later ceremony time. This would be listed 30 minutes after the ceremony starts, making a 2:00 pm drinks reception.

If your wedding is taking place in a church then some guests may then have to travel to your reception venue, this time needs to be taken into consideration too. When choosing your ceremony and reception venue you should be mindful of the distance between the two as you don't want guests to spend a long time travelling. This will just eat into your day and leave you short of time for all the exciting stuff!

During the drinks reception, your guests will be enjoying their time socialising with others. Your photographer may well take you away at this point to have some photos taken too, or they may do some group shots depending on what you require.

There will always be exceptions to the average order of the day, some of you may not have certain elements that we are including, and some may have more, just work it out around your schedule if this is the case.

Wedding Breakfast: 4:30 pm

On average a drinks reception lasts around 2/2.5 hours before guests start to take their seats for the wedding breakfast. Once your guests sit down for their wedding breakfast they will stay here for a good while. This is why we need to make sure it is comfortable for them. Depending on what you serve your guests I would allow two hours for the wedding breakfast.

Speeches: 6:30 pm

Speeches then normally take place at the end of your wedding breakfast. Depending on how many people make a speech, will determine how much time you allow for this part of the day. I would say a maximum of half an hour is needed. Guests will start to get restless and want to stretch their legs. They will have some time at this point to have a quick freshen-up and get some air, before the day turns into the evening.

Evening Guests Arrive: 7:00 pm

If you have invited more guests for your evening party then this is normally the next step outlined on your order of the day. It is important that your wedding breakfast does not overrun, the last thing you would want is more guests arriving before the day guests have finished eating.

Cake Cutting/First Dance: 7:45 pm

Once your evening guests have settled in, the next step is the cutting of your wedding cake which is followed by your first dance. These two events often get put together on an order of the day as they happen quite quickly one after another. Normally after cutting your wedding cake you get swept onto the dance floor for that all important first dance.

Evening Food: 9:00 pm

As you continue through the evening you may want to provide more food for your guests to enjoy, this is normally offered around 9:00 pm. However, it is best to be led by your caterer for advice on this.

Home Time/ Carriages: 12:00 am

Lastly, it is always a good idea to tell people what time you expect them to leave, if they need to book transport home then they know what time to schedule this for. The majority of venues will stop at midnight so it is important this is outlined on your order of the day.

These steps should give you a good indication of how to schedule your order of the day, your start time is always your ceremony time and your end time is always the time the venue wants you to stop. All your events need to fit comfortably between these two times. Discuss your timeline with your venue and your caterers to make sure it works for everyone. They will be able to advise you to make sure it all runs smoothly.

Make Notes
ORDER OF THE DAY

Area 03

CARDS & GIFTS

I know many of you will have asked your guests not to bring you physical gifts, and many of you would much prefer actual money or vouchers to be placed into your cards. There is no shame in that at all, traditional gifts like kettles and toasters are not so popular these days. I think the modern world is so different now. Many couples have already set up their homes with all they need to have filled them, long before their wedding day. Instead, I know you would be more grateful for money to be gifted, so you can put it towards your honeymoon or something of your own choice to purchase.

I hate to tell you, but your guests will still bring you gifts, possibly as well as give you money though too, so all is not lost. Even if it's something small, guests like to be seen to be giving. This is in return for your gesture of sharing your day with them, so the sentiment is quite sweet.

The chosen area for your guests' gestures needs to be close to where your guests first arrive. They will not want to sit or stand with things in their hands for long periods. You need them to put them somewhere, so they are then free to relax and enjoy a drink ahead of your Ceremony.

CARDS & GIFTS

The majority of venues will provide you with a simple clothed table near the arrival door for cards and presents to be placed on.

You will just need to choose some form of postbox for your cards to be securely placed in. I have used many things for this job before, such as crates and suitcases, we even once used a converted doll's house. You may have something at home already that you could use for your postbox, like a basket, or a champagne bowl, look at how you could utilise something to work for you.

One major factor to be mindful of when choosing your postbox is that potentially your wedding cards could have lots of money in them. For this reason, many couples will want to opt for a box with a lock on it, so everything is kept safe. This is why traditional postboxes are such a popular choice.

CARDS & GIFTS

This table will very quickly fill with gifts from your loved ones, but it is nice to add a little personalisation to it too. A few photographs or some flowers in small bud vases will just lift this table and make it more pleasing to the eye.

If you have opted for a postbox that is not regular, then sometimes guests will need a little encouragement to use something that maybe is not being used for its original purpose. They will be suspicious and will not want to make themselves look silly by assuming they know what to do. I would make it clear for them by leaving instructions or a little quotation for them, so they cannot go wrong.

Make Notes
CARDS & GIFTS

Area 04

THE CEREMONY

This moment in time is going to stay in your head and your heart forever. It will be a big deal to say those all-important vows to your new spouse. I know many of my brides-to-be say that this is the part of their wedding day they spend daydreaming about the most.

This is the next important area to consider when decorating and could potentially look different for each of you. One thing I will say is that although this is an important part of your wedding day, it is also the shortest part of the whole day. On average a wedding ceremony only lasts between 20-30 minutes.

Lots of my clients forget that this room is only used for a very short time. They also forget that it will not ever be empty. It will be full of people who are all in their beautiful attire. Before you decide how to decorate this room, be mindful of it being full of people, it will change your perspective of how to dress it. It is the people that will make this area of your wedding come alive.

THE CEREMONY

The seating is always the best place to start in this area and if any decoration is required on them. It is not always essential to decorate all of your ceremony chairs. Quite often I only decorate the aisle chairs, or the back row, as these are the ones that are most visual upon entering the ceremony area. If you are getting married in a church then pew ends are quite popular to use.

Try to think practically about this area and how people will move around it, it can make a big difference to where things can be placed. Walkways or aisles should not be cluttered with trip hazards.

Moving your decor up to eye level can be beneficial rather than having it at floor height. The last thing you want to happen is that someone trips over, or decorations get damaged.

THE CEREMONY

Guests may appreciate being told if there is a seating plan during the ceremony. Signage can be used for this, or you can just make sure your Ushers are on hand to settle people into the space comfortably. If you want to reserve seating for your main wedding party, then reserved seating signs can be placed on the first few rows of chairs. Guests appreciate you being clear with them, so they don't end up in the wrong place and feel awkward.

THE CEREMONY

Look around you to see what other decoration is required in this space. Everyone's eyes should be on you at the front of the room. Don't be daunted by this, embrace it, you are making memories for your eternity. I promise it's not as nerve-racking as you imagine, more emotional, so make sure someone does have a tissue on hand for you.

You can highlight your area by adding a backdrop, like a wedding arch or something similar. All your decoration needs to be balanced with what else is going on in this space too, bear this in mind when you visualise your ceremony.

Many ceremonies will have a table at the top of the aisle, this is where you will sign your wedding registration forms. Any decoration that you use on this table can be reused. A secret in the trade is to transfer this decor from your ceremony room to your reception room and onto your top table after the ceremony has finished. Re-purposing and reusing any of your decor around the venue is a great way to save you money.

THE CONFETTI THROW

Confetti is something that couples should now provide for their guests for after their ceremony. Traditionally guests would bring this with them, but due to sustainability many venues will require you to use and provide biodegradable confetti. It would be worthwhile checking your venue's policy about confetti before you make any decisions about it.

If confetti is allowed at your venue, then I think that you need to be considerate in choosing how to display your confetti too. Plastic boxes and paper cones all look lovely, but they just create further waste, that your guests will not know how to dispose of.

Popping your confetti into a basket for guests to take a handful of, is in my opinion the easiest way to contain it. You can keep it secure and dry in a tupperware box right up until you need it. Then one of your bride tribe can simply empty it out into a basket or something similar when it is required. This is good for the environment, good for your budget and good for your guests too!

Alternatives can also be used, such as bubbles or a sparkler send off!

Make Notes

THE CEREMONY

Area 05
THE RECEPTION

This is the largest of all the areas that will require wedding decoration at your venue. The one where the majority of time is spent.

A very good place to start when considering this area is with your wedding breakfast tables. What shape of table you will use and how many tables you will require, is really useful information to know before planning any further. When you visit a stylist or consider your decoration, this decision is vital to going forward and making plans.

Wedding venues on average will advise that you should sit between 8-10 people per standard 5'9" round guest table.

My personal opinion is that 8 people per round table is ample, guests will not want to feel hemmed in. However, it sometimes isn't always possible to have the perfect number on each table, but it is helpful to work on 8 people per table to start with.

If you opt for long trestle tables, these are normally 6' long and will seat 3 people on either side.

TIP

A quick calculation of how many tables you need -

To work out how many tables you will require, simply take the total number of daytime wedding guests and minus the number of people who will be sitting at your Top Table. Divide this remaining amount by 8 and this will give you the number of tables you will need.

It will give you a good starting point of how many tables will require decoration. If your calculation is not a whole number, I would round it up.
It is always easier to get rid of a table rather than have to add an extra one.
.

Example: A wedding seating 100 guests, with 12 people on the top table, means 11 round guest tables will be required.

THE RECEPTION

Before deciding how to decorate your wedding reception room, I would take into account some simple things.

For example
The size of the room
The colour or colours already present in the room
The height of the ceiling
The layout of the room

Your first thoughts should be focused on the purpose of the room, what you need it to do and who will be using it. These are really important points that could have a bearing on the overall decoration used.

THE RECEPTION

This is another very good time to put your wedding guests' needs first. It can help you create a good plan of action.

You want your guests to be able to:

- Easily locate and make their way to their table and chairs.
- Sit comfortably and see each other without their view being blocked.
- Be able to reach their food and drink easily, however it is served.
- Be able to sit their chair back and see the top table when the speeches are being delivered.

Keeping your guests at the forefront of your decisions will help them enjoy their time with you on your big day.

THE RECEPTION

Top Table

The top table is your VIP table, full of your favourite people. That may just include you and your spouse or it may be the full traditional lineup. Modern families aren't always made up of the perfect lineup, so just make it work for you and whatever feels most comfortable for your family dynamics.

Whoever joins you, you can easily make them feel a little extra special here. Requesting or sourcing something different for your top table can be a nice touch. An extra special wedding favour, a change in crockery or glassware can make all the difference.

As daunting as it can sound, you should be the real centre of attention on this table. Believe me when I say it is a nice place to be. Many couples will complement this table further by introducing a backdrop behind them or something in front of them.

I would always advise that whatever you do, you should avoid blocking anyone's view, or leaving big voids in the tablecloth. Your photographer will take many pictures of you whilst you are sitting here, be sure not to overlook the decoration. In years to come, you do not want to look back at photos and regret neglecting this table.

THE RECEPTION

Guest Tables

No matter what shape tables you choose for your guests to sit at, you need to be mindful of what the purpose of the table is. Your guests will be sitting here for quite a while during the wedding breakfast, they need to be comfortable during this time. You need to think practically, as well as think about all the pretty.

Each Table Requires

A table cloth
A centrepiece
A table name, or number
Guest name place
Napkins
Cutlery
Glassware

The majority of venues will supply you with plain white linens, cutlery and glassware. Anything extra is normal for you to supply. Of course, you can always change anything they provide if you wish, it all depends on how far you want to go. Coloured linens, like napkins, are becoming more popular in recent years. They are a good way to introduce more colour to your tables.

THE RECEPTION

Centrepieces
Before you can decide on what you wish to place in the centre of your tables for decoration, some things need to be considered.

Flowers
It is always good to think about your desire for flowers and what your budget is for them. If flowers are your thing, then this should be the focal point of your centrepiece. Be mindful that the bigger the vessel you use for your flowers, the more flowers you will require and therefore raise the overall cost. If you opt for smaller vessels, like bottles and bud vases then fewer flowers will be required, reducing your flower costs.

Consistency
When decorating any part of your wedding, it is important to create consistency. If you start with a rustic wedding ceremony and then move on to a boho reception it leaves guests feeling a little unsettled. Try to stay consistent throughout the whole day with your theme and also your colour palette. This will keep guests comfortable and relaxed.

THE RECEPTION

Food Choice
If you are serving food from sharing platters you need to make sure that your centrepiece allows enough room around it for these to be laid on the table. You don't want to have things disturbed and pushed to the side to make room for food to be placed on the table.

The Height Of The Ceiling
If you are in a room that has a high ceiling then using tall centrepieces can complement this. Anything too low will get lost on your tables and be swallowed up by things like wine bottles and water jugs. Think of the room's overall look after it's been decorated, don't just focus your attention on one table that is not completely dressed.

Candles
For safety reasons many venues no longer allow candles to be lit. This can change your view on a candle-heavy centrepiece, like a candelabra or cylinder vase. This isn't the case for all venues, but it is important, you must ask this question before you make any decision.

THE RECEPTION

Chairs

Next, it is time to turn your thoughts to the chairs that will be used around your tables.

Many of you with beady eyes will have probably clocked your venue's chairs early on when you first visited. The majority of modern venues will supply chairs that do not necessarily require any decoration. With an older venue you may not always have this luxury, some chairs I am afraid will need some attention. If you are thinking of using chair covers, it could also be worth considering outsourcing different chairs altogether as an alternative, surprisingly the cost can be quite similar.

Just like your ceremony area, it could be the case that decoration on each chair isn't always required. Every other chair could be decorated instead, this would make you a saving on your budget and can often soften the overall decor too.

THE RECEPTION

Table Plan

A table plan is something that I believe is always required with large numbers of guests. I don't think it's worth leaving it to chance where people will sit. Having a little order and control over this is a good thing.

I know sometimes it can be a difficult task to make decisions on who should sit where, due to family dynamics, but it is worth taking the time to make sure you have your say on this.

There will naturally be some sort of pecking order to your tables, you will want to have those close family members sitting nearer to you, then maybe those work colleagues that you see in the office every day.

Once you have decided on who should sit where you then need to decide how to display this so everyone can see. Whatever decision you make, you need it to be clear. Potentially you could have 100, or more people staring at this, so fonts need to be clear and visible. The table plan should be placed somewhere near your wedding breakfast room, so guests have this information before heading in.

Quick

TIP

How to work out your table plan -

Cut a circle out of some card that is approximately 20cm wide. One circle will represent one wedding breakfast table, so you will need to cut out as many circles as you expect to have tables in your wedding reception room. If you are having long tables then cut out rectangles instead.

Next get a fresh packet of wooden clothes pegs, the ones with the springs, that clip on. Take a pen and write each of your guests' names on each of the sides of the wooden pegs. Then peg your chosen guests onto the round card table.
This will give you a good opportunity to play about with who should sit where, without going through lots of paper and drawing out numerous options, as that will just cause you confusion. This way it will be clearer to see not only who is sitting where, but whose tables will be next to each other, giving you an overall view of the whole room.

THE RECEPTION

After decorating your tables, take a look around the rest of this room and decide if you need to add anything further.

Each of your reception rooms will be different and will look different depending on how many guests you intend to fill it with.

I have learnt that very small decorations will easily be swallowed up in a large room. If you intend to add something, then make sure it is worth the effort and it will be noticed.

You also need to try to avoid creating anything that may cause a hazard, for instance, if you are hanging things from a ceiling make sure they are at a height that people won't have to duck underneath them.

All your decoration needs to be worth the value and the labour, if something is really labour intensive then you need to make sure that it adds enough to the look to make that effort worthwhile. Likewise with cost, if you find yourself wanting something that is rather costly, make sure the want is great enough to warrant the spend. This is true of all your decoration throughout your whole day, not just in the reception room. Looking at your budget and your desire for something will help you work out what is essential to you and what is not essential.

Quick

TIP

Bouquets -

I have never known a wedding without a bouquet. Every bride I have worked with has always had one to accompany her and her bridesmaids. Bouquets don't necessarily have to be made from flowers. My bouquet was made up of family brooches, there are many variants from just flowers. However, I think it is important that we get value for money from all our bouquets and these should be shown off throughout the day, not just held during the ceremony.

I tell all of my couples that they should provide vases for bouquets to be placed in when they are no longer being used. Not only will this enhance your decoration, but it will mean that in the following days after your wedding you will be able to admire your flowers and perhaps dry them to keep as a memento from your big day.

THE RECEPTION

Once the wedding breakfast is over, your room may then need to be turned around for your evening celebrations. Sometimes some tables will have to be removed to make space for your dance floor area.

It is not always the case, but if tables are removed, then perhaps consider asking your venue to use the decorations elsewhere. Look out for bay windows, or maybe even outside tables that will be used during the evening. Try not to let it go to waste, anything you can reutilise is a good thing, rather than things being packed away early.

Evening time is also a good opportunity to bring out more lights, if like me you are a lover of fairy lights and the twinkle they bring, then think where and how these could be utilised. Empty fireplaces or mantlepieces are good areas for some extra lights. Windowsills or the Bar area are also nice places to add extra light. As long as you aren't causing obstructions then they will enhance the evening light. I often use battery fairy lights, so I am not reliant on plug sockets and don't have to worry about creating trip hazards.

THE RECEPTION

As I mentioned at the beginning, this room is the main area of the day. Your guests will have made themselves at home a bit more now they are well-fed, lubricated and feel more comfortable in their surroundings.

Once the room is ready for the evening you may have more guests due to arrive, do not feel you need to add more chairs for these guests. There won't be a point where this is now required, or needed.

No one now needs to be in a set place, guests can get up and socialise with others outside of their tables. The room needs to be workable for people to dance and use the bar. It now becomes a nice social space for all to enjoy.

You may choose to add a more comfortable, or quieter area for people to sit but it isn't necessarily required. Try not to segregate people too much or you will lose the atmosphere.

Make Notes

THE RECEPTION

Make Notes

THE RECEPTION

Area 06
THE CAKE

The cutting of the wedding cake is a relatively old tradition, but it remains very much part of a modern wedding day too.

Usually, you will cut your cake in the evening, before that all-important first dance. This may need to be taken into consideration when you are thinking about where your cake should be located. Then you can sweep yourselves effortlessly onto the dance floor afterwards.

One big tip that I have learnt over my years in the industry, is that a cake should never be placed near a window in the summer months, they don't like it very much! That doesn't mean it needs to be pushed into a corner either, but just be mindful of where you do want it to be located and what time of day it is on display.

THE CAKE

The majority of venues will supply you with a round table for your cake to sit on, which is approximately 3' in diameter.

Some venues may also say that they will supply you with a cake stand too, but do make sure that this matches the rest of your decor, as well as the cake itself.

If you purchase your cake stand then do make sure it is up to the job. Wedding cakes can be extremely heavy, you do not want them to buckle under the pressure.

The decoration around your cake table or stand is completely a personal choice. Sometimes, it is nice to use a sparkly tablecloth or a jazzy cake stand. Whatever you decide, it is always a good idea to have a discussion with your cake maker about it, they will know what will work best with their creation.

Make Notes
THE CAKE

Area 07
GUEST SIGNING

A guest signing area is a space where your guests can leave messages of appreciation and love for you on your wedding day.

Just be mindful that whatever you get your guests to sign, it is something that you keep long after your wedding day. I always try to encourage all my clients to not just use a book for this. In my experience after your wedding day is over, you can feel a little blue about it all. It is a day that has had your attention for months, if not years, so when it is over it can feel very strange to release all of those thoughts. With this in mind, it is important that you have some amazing physical tokens from your wedding day. Things that you can treasure forever. That is why, in my opinion, a book just doesn't do all those lovely messages justice.

A book will be closed and left to collect dust on a shelf somewhere and barely seen. Think beyond a book, a jigsaw, or a picture, you only have to look on Pinterest for lots of creative options. Just make it something that can be appreciated more frequently, something that can be hung up and admired every day. Trust me on this, as years from now, you will appreciate this decision.

Make Notes
GUEST SIGNING

Bringing it All together

Once you have gone through each of my steps and considered what decor you would like to choose for each of these areas, it is really important to make sure that your choices complement each other. When you design your wedding style you create your very own brand and like every good brand it will come with consistency. Your wedding guests become accustomed to your chosen colours, fonts and even your flower choices. If you can achieve continuity throughout your whole day, then guests are much more relaxed. Being comfortable in the environment that they are present in will create contentment and comfort. In turn, this means that guests are far more likely to have more fun and enjoy the fantastic day you have created.

It will also make your life far easier too, blending different themes can be tricky, so make things simpler by sticking to the same feel throughout. From your invitations to your thank you cards and everything else in between, your styling should be the same, this is key to nailing your very own wedding brand.

Make your own
WED-BOARD

If you are struggling to narrow down your options of what decoration to use, it can be really useful to make yourself a mood board or two!

I do these for my Facebook groupies who need some clarification on what they are trying to create. Bringing your ideas together can help your mind settle on lots of things but mainly a colour scheme and a theme. You will be able to see how your choices complement one another and if any adjustments may be needed.

HOW TO MAKE A WED-BOARD

Like many people that come to visit me, you have probably made quite a collection of what I like to call wed-spiration photos on your phone.

Pinterest, Google and Instagram are all great places to source inspiration for your wedding day, but sometimes your photos can get jumbled and end up a bit unorganised. This can make your thoughts about what you are trying to achieve become disorganised too. Keeping your photos in order is a great way of keeping your thoughts in order. Try to pop things into albums rather than letting everything merge.

For example
Wedding Hair
Wedding Stationery
Wedding Tables

To make your mood board choose five or six photos from different areas of your wedding or your newly organised albums and then simply put them together. Canva is a really simple app that you can download to your phone. It's available to use for free to do simple tasks on, like making mood boards. If you are a techno-phobe like me I promise it is easy to use. Once you start to get a bit more comfortable with it you can then start to add coloured backgrounds to it or go as far as adding graphics. It doesn't matter how fancy or not you go, the main result is that you have something you can use as a reference. Something you can relate to when choosing through endless options. This will make sure you are keeping in line with what you want to design. You can also share your moodboard to potential suppliers too. This will enable them to quickly get a feel for what you are trying to create.

Enjoying your day

It sounds crazy that I need to tell you to enjoy your wedding day, but all too often I see couples burn themselves out before their day even arrives. This purely comes from taking on too much.

All of you will be juggling normal life alongside your wedding planning. As the day gets closer, the demands naturally increase. All your friends and family will be gearing themselves up for preparations and you can easily start to feel like you are being pulled in different directions.

For some couples they will take this all in their stride, for others, it can all get a bit much. Taking on wedding planning, preparation and decoration is rather a lot to contend with. Make sure you offload some of the burdens. This maybe to family or it maybe to friends or may even mean hiring help. Whatever you choose just make sure you are not running yourself ragged.

I always explain to my clients that your wedding day is just like Christmas. It isn't just about the actual day, of course this is a once in a lifetime day, but the whole run up and planning as well as your wedding eve should all be great fun too. Allow youself to enjoy all aspects of your big day.

Relieving
the stress

Decorating your venue for your wedding day is not something that should be rushed. If your venue is only allowing you to decorate on the morning of your wedding then I would strongly advise that you delegate the decorating to someone else. Discuss with your venue what your options are and if this is something they would do for you. Some venues are happy to help, others will advise you to hire assistance.

Many of my couples have chosen to do it themselves and they've always told me afterwards that they wish they hadn't. That it spoilt their morning and that the stress of sorting it all was too much. They wished they had been able to give this responsibility to someone they trusted. Some of you may worry about the cost of hiring someone, but for a professional, it will only take a few hours and the cost will be a very small percentage of the rest of the wedding. It will not only relieve your time and stress levels but it will also give you the confidence to know it will all be done perfectly.

You will be far too busy to undertake such a task anyway, your hair and makeup take quite a long time and the last thing you want to be doing is running around sorting out centrepieces.

The Days After

I know no one ever really discusses their wedding Boxing Day before their actual wedding day, but it is a good idea to have a bit of a plan in your head of logistically what you may need to do.

There is always a bit of cleaning up the following day at the venue, I don't necessarily mean physical cleaning, but you will have to return to collect any of your belongings. Make sure your cars are empty on your return, you will need the space ready to fill them up. Everything you took with you, will now need to come back, as well as presents people have gifted, leftover wedding cake and all your flowers.

Consider returning with a few boxes to collect things up with and possibly even a bucket to put flowers in. They are all very practical considerations, but you will thank me for them when the day arrives. You could well be feeling a little fragile, so the easier you can make your lives, the better.

To avoid taking home lots of flower arrangements, consider gifting some of them to family or friends.

THE DAYS AFTER

After all the clearing-up is done and you have caught up on some sleep, it can then all feel a little bit strange. By strange I mean you may feel a little lost, the whole wedding day run-up has had your full attention for so long, that once it is all over it can leave you feeling a little low.

It takes a while to digest all of the excitement that has just happened and to find a little bit of normality again. You will question yourselves over what it was you used to spend your time thinking about.

I am only sharing this with you because I found it hard to just believe our day was over. We had such a fabulous time and I enjoyed the planning and the preparations so much, that I did feel a little lost afterwards.

It is important to keep your focus on something positive. Maybe some time away like your honeymoon, minimoon or even a weekend off together to be able to gather your thoughts is a good idea.

THE DAYS AFTER

This is also why I believe it is so important to have given yourselves lovely keepsakes from the day and also why it is important to have invested in a great photographer who will have captured all your amazing memories. If you can stretch that little bit further to a videographer then do not hesitate. Imagine in 30 years someone saying you could watch your whole wedding day again with your children or maybe even your grandchildren, then I think you would all jump at the chance.

Thank You

I am hoping that my simple styling guide has made this whole area of your wedding much clearer. At this point, I want you to feel that you can now go forth and work out what decoration is required. Having a practical approach to your wedding decoration will streamline the whole process for you and make your life simpler.

Take one step at a time and do not rush it, you are likely to have time on your side, so make your decisions carefully.

I would love to see how your wedding day decoration plans are going and of course, I would love to see the final results. Please do send us any photographs of what you create, or even how you created it. I would also really welcome any reviews of our Simple Guide and how it helps you to create your dream day. Please do share this guide with anyone else that may need some help too. Please share on your socials and tag us so we can see how you are all getting on. Planning a wedding is a journey and one that should be enjoyed. It isn't always easy, but together we can make it simpler.

Thank You

All the photographs are of my own clients' weddings, taken by the fabulously talented Lee Daniels Photography. A huge thank you to him and my wonderful couples for letting me share their photos.

Lisa & Gordon

Marrissa & Pete

Sophie & Thomas

Samantha & Lucas

Becky & Carl

Get Social

🌐 www.prettyquirkyhire.co.uk

📷 Pretty Quirky Hire

f The Savvy Wedding Journey

f Pretty Quirky

▶ Prettyquirkyweddings

Printed in Poland
by Amazon Fulfillment
Poland Sp. z o.o., Wrocław

17219713R10049